The 36 Stratagems For Beginners

+ 36 Practical Tips

+ 36 Practical Exercises

Copyright © August 2024

"The 36 Stratagems for Beginners"

Publisher: Createspace Independently Published

ISBN-13: 9798337637020

Copying or any other form of total or partial reproduction of the text is prohibited without the author's permission.

Image: This cover was designed using resources from Freepik.com.

TABLE OF CONTENTS

INTRODUCTION	1
THE 36 STRATAGEMS WITH ADVICE	6
I. Stratagems for Victory (When you are in a position of strength)	6
II. Stratagems for Confrontation (When you are in a position of parity)	9
III. Stratagems for Attacking (When you are in a position of strength)	12
IV. Stratagems for Retreating (When you are in a position of weakness)	15
V. Stratagems for Melee (When you are in an uncertain position)	18
VI. Stratagems for Desperation (When you have no choice)	21
36 EXERCISES TO PUT INTO PRACTICE	25
PERSONAL TESTIMONIES	37
THE SECRET OF HAPPINESS	43
HOW TO APPLY THE 36 STRATAGEMS TO ACHIEVE HAPPINESS	47
CONCLUSIONS/ACKNOWLEDGMENTS	61

INTRODUCTION

In a rapidly evolving world, where the complexity of daily challenges sometimes seems to overwhelm us, ancient wisdom can offer a surprisingly accurate compass. The 36 Chinese stratagems, a treasure trove of cunning and strategy passed down through the centuries, represent just such a compass: a compendium of tactics and principles that, despite their origin in ancient China, resonate with extraordinary relevance in our contemporary context.

This book aims to be more than a simple collection of ancient maxims. It is a bridge between the past and the present, a practical manual for navigating the tumultuous waters of modern life armed with the wisdom of millennia. Through these pages, we will embark on a three-stage journey, each designed to deepen our understanding and application of these timeless principles.

In the first part of the book, we will explore each of the 36 stratagems in detail. From 'Deceive the sky to cross the sea' to 'Tie the grass to catch the rabbit', each stratagem will be analyzed in its historical context, unveiling the subtle nuances of meaning hidden behind these enigmatic phrases. We will discover how these principles were applied on the battlefields of ancient China, but also how they have influenced politics, business, and even the arts over the centuries.

But the true strength of these stratagems lies in their universal applicability. That's why, in the second part of the book, we will present 36 practical tips, each inspired by a specific stratagem. These tips ferry ancient wisdom into the 21st century, offering concrete solutions to contemporary challenges. We will learn how 'Hide a knife behind a smile' can translate into effective negotiation techniques, or how 'Sacrifice the plum tree to save the peach tree' can guide us in difficult business decisions.

However, knowledge without practice remains sterile. For this reason, the third and final part of the book is dedicated to action. For each stratagem, we will propose a practical exercise, designed to internalize and concretely apply these principles in daily life. These exercises will range from personal reflection to scenario simulation, from case study analysis to the practice of specific techniques. The goal is to transform ancient wisdom into tangible and applicable skills.

This book is not just a text to read, but an experience to live. It is an invitation to explore the depths of strategy and cunning, to challenge one's perceptions and to develop a sharper and more versatile mindset. Whether you are business leaders looking for a competitive edge, students eager to excel in your studies, or simply individuals seeking a richer and more conscious life, you will find valuable tools for your journey in these pages.

As we immerse ourselves in the fascinating world of the 36 stratagems, let us remember that true wisdom lies not in the mere accumulation of knowledge, but in its ethical and thoughtful application. These stratagems, born in an era of conflicts and intrigues, teach us not only the art of strategy, but also the importance of balance, flexibility, and deep understanding of human dynamics.

Prepare yourself for a journey that will challenge your way of thinking, broaden your horizons, and provide you with powerful tools to face the challenges of modern life. From the battlefields of ancient China to today's boardrooms, from diplomatic conflicts to personal relationships, the wisdom of the 36 stratagems continues to illuminate the path of those seeking excellence and mastery in their own lives.

THE 36 STRATAGEMS

Welcome to a world where deception can be virtue, weakness can hide strength, and where true victory often resides not in brute force, but in the subtle art of strategy. Welcome to the timeless world of the 36 Chinese stratagems, now more relevant than ever in our complex contemporary landscape.

THE 36 STRATAGEMS WITH ADVICE

I. Stratagems for Victory (When you are in a position of strength)

1. Deceptive Deception

   - Stratagem: Do something surprising to draw the enemy's attention to a trap.

   - Advice for daily life: In a competitive context, such as a negotiation or deal, propose a seemingly advantageous solution that benefits you more. This can push the other party to focus on a minor detail while you get what you want.

2. Make Noise in the East and Attack in the West

   - Stratagem: Create chaos to confuse the enemy and strike at an unexpected point.

- Advice for daily life: When you need to achieve something without drawing too much attention, distract others with secondary activities or information that keeps them busy, while you discreetly reach your main goal.

3. Surprise Assault to Take the Stronghold

- Stratagem: Concentrate your forces to achieve a decisive victory.

- Advice for daily life: When you want to tackle an important task, plan carefully and focus on it without distractions. A determined and well-prepared action can lead to decisive success, such as completing a crucial project or getting a promotion.

4. Rest While the Enemy Tires

- Stratagem: Wear out the enemy while keeping your own forces intact.

- Advice for daily life: In competitive contexts, such as at work or in sports, don't waste your energy immediately. Let others wear themselves out while you wisely manage your energy. Wait for the right moment to act with strength.

5. Plunder an Empty House

- Stratagem: Attack when the enemy is in a moment of vulnerability.

- Advice for daily life: Take advantage of opportunities when others are distracted or not at their best. For example, seize the chance to propose an idea or ask for a favor when your interlocutor is more likely to accept.

6. Create Something from Nothing

- Stratagem: Confuse the enemy by creating illusions and false appearances.

- Advice for daily life: When you need to obtain something or influence a decision, create a positive perception of yourself or your proposal. Sometimes, the presentation of an idea or self-image can be just as important as the substance itself.

II. Stratagems for Confrontation (When you are in a position of parity)

7. Strike with a Hidden Blade

- Stratagem: Appear harmless to strike the enemy by surprise.

- Advice for daily life: When working on a project or proposal, avoid revealing all your ideas immediately. Wait for the right moment to unveil your winning move, so as to gain an unexpected advantage.

8. Borrow a Sword to Kill

- Stratagem: Use others' resources to fight on your behalf.

- Advice for daily life: If you need to achieve a result, consider collaborating with those who have the necessary skills or resources. This way, you can reach your goal without having to do everything alone.

9. Advance Quickly to Find a Safe Position

- Stratagem: Exploit the right moment to take initiative and capture the enemy.

- Advice for daily life: If you notice an opportunity that might close quickly, act without hesitation. Being ready to seize the moment can make the difference between success and failure.

10. Remove the Logs to Drown the Fish

- Stratagem: Weaken the enemy's base to make them ineffective.

- Advice for daily life: In a discussion or negotiation, identify the central argument or support of the other party. If you can weaken that point, their position will lose strength, giving you an advantage.

11. Beat the Grass to Startle the Snakes

- Stratagem: Provoke the enemy to discover their intentions.

- Advice for daily life: When you suspect someone is hiding something, make a move that forces them to reveal themselves. For example, ask a direct question or propose an action that puts them to the test.

12. Beat the Snake with a Stick

- Stratagem: Strike the enemy when they are in an unfavorable position.

- Advice for daily life: If someone is in difficulty or has made a mistake, act promptly to ensure you benefit from it. For example, if a competitor has a moment of weakness, seize the opportunity to strengthen your position.

III. Stratagems for Attacking (When you are in a position of strength)

13. Deceptive Retreat to Strike

- Stratagem: Feign a retreat to lure the enemy into a trap.

- Advice for daily life: If you find yourself in a difficult situation, it can be useful to take a step back to reorganize. Sometimes, pretending to surrender or retreat can induce others to reveal their true intentions, giving you time to prepare a stronger response.

14. Flee with the Enemy in Flames

- Stratagem: Create an opening to escape when you're in a desperate situation.

- Advice for daily life: When you find yourself in a situation with no way out, try to create an unexpected solution or escape route. This could mean changing strategy or finding an alternative that allows you to avoid the worst.

15. Throw a Brick to Get a Jade

- Stratagem: Offer something small to gain a great advantage.

- Advice for daily life: Sometimes, it's necessary to make a small concession or sacrifice to obtain something bigger. For example, granting a minor request could help you get a more advantageous deal in the future.

16. Absorb Energy to Take the Upper Hand

- Stratagem: Use the enemy's strength against them.

- Advice for daily life: If someone attacks or criticizes you, try to use their words or actions to your advantage. This could mean turning a criticism into an opportunity to improve or to demonstrate your value.

17. Throw Meat to Distract the Tiger

- Stratagem: Use a false opportunity to distract the enemy.

- Advice for daily life: When you need to buy time or shift attention from something important, offer a distraction or alternative that seems attractive. This will allow you to focus on what's truly important without interference.

18. Borrow a Sheep to Get Rich

- Stratagem: Exploit any opportunity to enrich yourself.

- Advice for daily life: Be ready to seize opportunities that present themselves, even if they seem small. Even minor resources or unexpected occasions can lead to significant gains if used correctly.

IV. Stratagems for Retreating (When you are in a position of weakness)

19. Strike at the Heart to Weaken the Spirit

- Stratagem: Attack the enemy's weak point to weaken them.

- Advice for daily life: When facing a challenge or a difficult person, identify their weak point or the key aspect that influences them the most. Focus on this element to solve the problem more effectively, rather than trying to tackle everything at once.

20. Strategic Retreat to Maintain Forces

- Stratagem: Retreat to avoid unnecessary losses and preserve forces.

- Advice for daily life: In stressful situations or when you feel overwhelmed, taking a break or temporarily distancing yourself can help you recharge and come back stronger. It's not always necessary to react immediately; sometimes, a strategic step back is the best choice.

21. Separation Tactics to Disorient the Enemy

- Stratagem: Divide enemy forces to make them easier to defeat.

- Advice for daily life: If you're working in a team or collaborative situation, try to divide tasks or manage conflicts by isolating problems. Separating conflicting parties can facilitate resolution and improve overall efficiency.

22. Set Fire to the Enemy on All Sides

- Stratagem: Attack simultaneously on multiple fronts to wear out the enemy.

- Advice for daily life: When tackling a project or challenge, consider working on multiple aspects simultaneously to accelerate progress. Distributing your energy across various tasks can lead to faster results and more effective time management.

23. Hide the Sword in a Smile

- Stratagem: Appear friendly while preparing for attack.

- Advice for daily life: Maintain a positive and friendly attitude even when working on personal or competitive goals. This allows you to build good relationships and gain trust, which can be useful when you need it most.

24. Attack from Afar While Defending Up Close

- Stratagem: Use long-range attacks to maintain distance from the enemy.

- Advice for daily life: Maintain a certain emotional or strategic distance in conflictual situations. Address problems indirectly or use resources that allow you to manage situations without exposing yourself too much, thus ensuring your safety and well-being.

V. Stratagems for Melee (When you are in an uncertain position)

25. Pay Attention to the Enemy's Forces

- Stratagem: Maintain control and vigilance over the enemy.

- Advice for daily life: Carefully observe people or situations that could represent a threat or challenge. Being aware of others' intentions and capabilities allows you to better prepare and avoid surprises.

26. Simulate Confusion to Capture the Enemy

- Stratagem: Feign disorganization to lure the enemy into a trap.

- Advice for daily life: In situations where you want to obtain information or observe others' reactions, you might pretend to be less prepared or confused. This can lead others to underestimate you or reveal something important.

27. See the Shadow to Avoid the Knives

- Stratagem: Be vigilant and prevent potential attacks.

- Advice for daily life: Be attentive to warning signs or small details that might indicate an impending problem. Anticipating potential risks allows you to avoid unpleasant or harmful situations.

28. Kill a Chicken to Scare the Monkeys

- Stratagem: Make an example to intimidate other enemies.

- Advice for daily life: In some cases, taking a firm stance against a small problem can send a clear message to others, discouraging further challenges or negative behaviors.

29. Replace the Shaky Column with a New One

- Stratagem: Renew what is weak or damaged.

- Advice for daily life: When something isn't working well, whether it's a habit, a project, or a relationship, consider replacing or renewing it. Investing in change can lead to a stronger foundation and better results.

30. Smiling Tactic to Hide True Intentions

- Stratagem: Feign sympathy while preparing for attack.

- Advice for daily life: Maintain a positive and open attitude even when you're planning something important. This allows you to keep your intentions private and act without raising suspicion, protecting your goals.

VI. Stratagems for Desperation (When you have no choice)

31. Use a Woman to Corrupt the Adversary

- Stratagem: Use seduction to distract or corrupt the enemy.

- Advice for daily life: It's not necessary to resort to seduction, but you can use charm and persuasion to positively influence others. Creating a pleasant environment and using charisma can help you get what you want in social or professional situations.

32. Open the Door to Invite the Enemy

- Stratagem: Create an opportunity to lure the enemy into a trap.

- Advice for daily life: When you want to manage a difficult situation, consider inviting the other party to talk or collaborate. Appearing open and available can lead others to underestimate your intentions, allowing you to better handle the situation.

33. Retreat to Gain New Strength

- Stratagem: Strategically retreat to reorganize and obtain a new opportunity to attack.

- Advice for daily life: When you find yourself in difficulty or a moment of stress, give yourself time to retreat and reflect. Taking a break can give you the strength and clarity needed to return with new ideas and solutions.

34. Hide Behind a Smile

- Stratagem: Pretend friendship while planning an attack.

- Advice for daily life: Maintain a positive and courteous attitude even when facing difficult situations. This allows you to protect your intentions and maintain healthy relationships while working towards your goals.

35. Escape Quickly When Surrounded

- Stratagem: Abandon the position when defeat is imminent.

- Advice for daily life: If you find yourself in a situation with no way out or where the odds are against you, don't hesitate to turn back or walk away. Knowing when it's time to leave is crucial to protect yourself and your resources.

36. Stratagem of the Collapsing Tower

- Stratagem: Destroy everything to leave nothing for the enemy if defeat is inevitable.

- Advice for daily life: If a project or situation is destined to fail, consider shutting everything down so as not to leave anything for others to exploit. Sometimes, it's better to start from scratch rather than let others take advantage of your failure.

EXERCISES TO PUT THE TEACHINGS INTO PRACTICE

We have created 36 practical exercises for you, one for each stratagem. Good work...

I. Stratagems for Victory

1. Deceptive Deception

 - Exercise: During a meeting or project, present a secondary idea that seems important but actually isn't. Observe how others focus on it while you work on the real objective.

2. Make Noise in the East and Attack in the West

 - Exercise: Plan your day by creating a distraction (like a less important task) for others while you focus on a crucial activity without interference.

3. Surprise Assault to Take the Stronghold

- Exercise: Identify an important task you've been postponing and complete it in a single day, surprising yourself and others with your efficiency.

4. Rest While the Enemy Tires

- Exercise: In a competitive situation, like a game or discussion, stay calm and conserve your energy while others wear themselves out. Act only when you're certain you have the advantage.

5. Plunder an Empty House

- Exercise: Take advantage of a moment of calm or lack of supervision to complete a task without distractions or interference.

6. Create Something from Nothing

- Exercise: Create a positive situation or opportunity for yourself starting from a small detail or resource that others might ignore.

II. Stratagems for Confrontation

7. Strike with a Hidden Blade

- Exercise: During a conversation, keep an important piece of information to yourself and reveal it only when it can have the maximum impact.

8. Borrow a Sword to Kill

- Exercise: Ask someone with specific skills for help to solve a problem for you, saving time and effort.

9. Advance Quickly to Find a Safe Position

- Exercise: Seize a sudden opportunity, like a job offer or event, by acting immediately to gain an advantage.

10. Remove the Logs to Drown the Fish

- Exercise: Identify the weak point of a problem and work directly on it to solve the entire issue.

11. Beat the Grass to Startle the Snakes

- Exercise: Ask a provocative question or propose an idea in a group to observe reactions and discover others' true intentions.

12. Beat the Snake with a Stick

- Exercise: Wait for a moment when someone is vulnerable (like after a mistake) and offer your help or solution to gain an advantage.

III. Stratagems for Attacking

13. Deceptive Retreat to Strike

- Exercise: In a discussion, temporarily retreat, let the other party relax, and then resume the discussion with new arguments.

14. Flee with the Enemy in Flames

- Exercise: When you're in trouble, seek a creative alternative to get out of a problematic situation instead of insisting on a path that doesn't work.

15. Throw a Brick to Get a Jade

- Exercise: Make a small concession in a negotiation to get something bigger in return.

16. Absorb Energy to Take the Upper Hand

- Exercise: If you receive criticism, use it to improve and demonstrate your value, turning an attack into an opportunity.

17. Throw Meat to Distract the Tiger

- Exercise: Offer a distraction or alternative when someone is focused on a problem, allowing you to solve another important issue without interference.

18. Borrow a Sheep to Get Rich

- Exercise: Find a way to exploit an available resource, even if small, to gain an advantage or profit.

IV. Stratagems for Retreating

19. Strike at the Heart to Weaken the Spirit

- Exercise: Identify the most critical aspect of a problem or situation and focus on that to solve it effectively.

20. Strategic Retreat to Maintain Forces

- Exercise: When you feel overwhelmed, take a break to recharge your energy and return with a clearer mind.

21. Separation Tactics to Disorient the Enemy

- Exercise: If you're managing a conflict or complex project, divide the problems into smaller parts and address them one at a time.

22. Set Fire to the Enemy on All Sides

- Exercise: Tackle an important project or task by managing multiple aspects simultaneously to achieve faster and more complete results.

23. Hide the Sword in a Smile

- Exercise: Maintain a friendly attitude even when you're working on something critical or preparing a strategic move.

24. Attack from Afar While Defending Up Close

- Exercise: Manage a difficult problem by maintaining emotional distance and seeking indirect or alternative solutions to reduce conflict.

V. Stratagems for Melee

25. Pay Attention to the Enemy's Forces

- Exercise: Carefully observe the people around you, especially those who might represent a challenge or threat, to better understand their intentions.

26. Simulate Confusion to Capture the Enemy

- Exercise: Pretend not to know or to be confused about a topic so that others relax and reveal more than they otherwise would.

27. See the Shadow to Avoid the Knives

- Exercise: Be attentive to danger signals or subtle details that could indicate an impending problem. Anticipate and act accordingly.

28. Kill a Chicken to Scare the Monkeys

- Exercise: In a group situation, address a small problem decisively to send a strong message to others.

29. Replace the Shaky Column with a New One

- Exercise: Identify a weak or ineffective part of your project or habit and replace it with something new and more solid.

30. Smiling Tactic to Hide True Intentions

- Exercise: Maintain a positive and courteous attitude even when you're planning something important or confidential, so as not to arouse suspicion.

VI. Stratagems for Desperation

31. Use a Woman to Corrupt the Adversary

- Exercise: Use charm and persuasion in a social or professional situation to positively influence the outcome.

32. Open the Door to Invite the Enemy

- Exercise: In a tense or conflictual situation, encourage the other party to dialogue or collaborate, creating an environment that seems advantageous to them but actually benefits you.

33. Retreat to Gain New Strength

- Exercise: If you're facing a series of failures, give yourself time to retreat, reflect, and reorganize before trying again.

34. Hide Behind a Smile

- Exercise: Maintain friendly and positive behavior even in stressful situations or when you're working towards a hidden goal.

35. Escape Quickly When Surrounded

- Exercise: If you find yourself in a situation with no way out or extremely unfavorable, abandon the situation and seek an immediate exit without regrets.

36. Stratagem of the Collapsing Tower

- Exercise: If a project or situation is inevitably destined to fail, consider shutting everything down definitively and plan to start over from scratch in a better context.

These exercises will help you integrate the ancient stratagems into your daily life.

PERSONAL TESTIMONIALS

We have selected 10 stories that demonstrate the effectiveness of the 36 stratagems. Enjoy reading!

1. Maria, tech entrepreneur (Stratagem: "Create Something from Nothing")

"When I launched my startup, I had no resources or connections. I used the stratagem 'Create Something from Nothing' to build a support network through social media. I created viral content that caught the attention of investors and partners. Today, my company is worth millions."

2. Luca, union negotiator (Stratagem: "Hide a Dagger Behind a Smile")

"During a difficult negotiation with corporate executives, I maintained a cordial and collaborative attitude, hiding my determination. This approach lowered their defenses, allowing me to secure significant concessions for the workers without creating a hostile atmosphere."

3. Sophia, university student (Stratagem: "Sacrifice the Plum Tree to Save the Peach Tree")

"When I realized that I couldn't excel in all my courses due to the workload, I decided to strategically focus on those most relevant to my future career. I 'sacrificed' some less important courses to excel in the key ones, significantly improving my job prospects."

4. Ahmed, department store manager (Stratagem: "Make a Sound in the East, Then Strike in the West")

"During the holiday season, I launched a big advertising campaign for our electronics products. While the competition focused on that, we quietly reorganized and strengthened our clothing department, which became the most profitable."

5. Elena, couples therapist (Stratagem: "Lend the Enemy a Knife")

"When couples are stuck in conflict, I often ask each partner to argue the other's point of view. This 'lending a knife' forces them to see the situation from a new perspective, often leading to breakthroughs in sessions."

6. Carlos, professional athlete (Stratagem: "Feign Madness But Keep Your Balance")

"During a crucial race, I pretended to be exhausted and demoralized. My opponent let his guard down, allowing me to surprise him with a burst of energy in the final stretch and win the competition."

7. Yuki, architect (Stratagem: "Pull the Firewood from Under the Cauldron")

"In a project that was going wrong, instead of abandoning it, I identified the salvageable elements. I redesigned the building around these elements, saving time and resources. The final result was an unexpected success."

8. David, middle school teacher (Stratagem: "Watch the Fire from the Other Side of the River")

"Instead of directly intervening in a conflict between students, I created situations where they had to collaborate. By observing their interactions, I understood the underlying dynamics and guided them toward a peaceful resolution without appearing authoritarian."

9. Amina, civil rights activist (Stratagem: "Hide a Sword in a Smile")

"In my campaigns, instead of directly attacking opposing politicians, I used humor and satire to highlight their contradictions. This approach made our message more accessible and increased public support for our cause."

10. Matteo, small business owner (Stratagem: "Take the Fuel Out of the Fire")

"When a larger competitor tried to invade my market, instead of competing directly, I identified and secured exclusive agreements with key suppliers. Without access to these suppliers, my competitor was unable to effectively establish themselves in my area."

These stories illustrate how the principles of the 36 stratagems can be applied creatively and ethically in various contexts of modern life, from entrepreneurship to education, from sports to social activism. Each testimonial shows how ancient wisdom can be reinterpreted to tackle contemporary challenges with ingenuity and strategy.

🖤 THE SECRET OF HAPPINESS 🖤

With these final words, I congratulate you on your reading journey and send you positive energy along with words that, if understood, will reveal the secret of happiness.

I may not know you personally, but I know for sure that you possess a powerful energy of white light within you. This is an inner strength that must be intensified, and if you understand the power of love, you will become invincible.

With these words, I want to help you understand the importance of doing good, first for yourself and then for others.

If you want to distance yourself from suffering and negativity and begin a path of serenity and happiness, there is one simple yet powerful secret: help and do good for everyone you encounter on your life's journey.

According to renowned psychologists, doing good for others triggers personal gratification and activates brain mechanisms linked to pleasure. These gratifications are so powerful that they reduce stress, boost self-esteem, and improve mood.

Moreover, altruism helps to create stronger and more genuine bonds with the people around you, strengthening your social connections.

Another reason is that it gives meaning to your life; being consistently altruistic provides you with a purpose, leading to personal fulfillment and, consequently, greater happiness.

But it doesn't stop there—other studies have confirmed that such practices positively impact mental health, directly working on depression and anxiety, promoting overall psychological well-being.

Let's not forget the "virtuous circle" effect, where your positive influence will inspire others, motivating them to reciprocate your actions with others, creating an endless chain of positive change.

I hope I've made you realize that you possess immense power within you, and this gift can be used for yourself and shared with others.

Start today: smile, do a good deed, make a small donation, help, share, listen, support, offer a kind word—all unconditionally.

Everyone has unique qualities; discover yours and use them to help those who cross your path.

Together, we can ignite a process of positive change in the world—starting today, now, in this moment.

Begin right away, and you will feel a rewarding sense of gratification. Changing the world starts with you. You have the power of love. Use it—we all need your light.

Now that you have understood the secret of happiness, embrace it and share it with others. The choice is yours alone.

I believe in you, and the world needs your love.

HOW TO APPLY THE 36 STRATAGEMS TO ACHIEVE HAPPINESS

Achieving happiness is a journey that requires awareness, commitment, and a deep love for yourself and others. The 36 stratagems, originally designed to overcome challenges and gain advantages in conflict situations, can be reinterpreted as tools to promote altruism and happiness, both for yourself and those around you. Here's how you can apply them to create a virtuous circle of positivity and well-being.

I. Stratagems for Victory

When you are in a position of strength, use them to illuminate the path for others and spread goodness.

1. Deceptive Trick

- Exercise: During a meeting or project, present a secondary idea that seems important but isn't. Observe how others focus on it while you work on the real goal.

2. Make a Noise in the East and Strike in the West

- Exercise: Plan your day by creating a distraction (like a less important task) for others while you focus on a crucial activity without interference.

3. Surprise Attack to Take the Stronghold

- Exercise: Identify an important task you've been putting off and complete it in a single day, surprising yourself and others with your efficiency.

4. Rest While the Enemy Exhausts Themselves

- Exercise: In a competitive situation, like a game or debate, stay calm and conserve energy while others exhaust themselves. Act only when you're sure of your advantage.

5. Loot a Burning House

- Exercise: Take advantage of a quiet moment or a lack of supervision to complete a task without distractions or interference.

6. Create Something from Nothing

- Exercise: Create a positive situation or opportunity for yourself from a small detail or resource that others might overlook.

II. Stratagems for Confrontation

When you are in a position of parity, apply these stratagems to build bridges of empathy and understanding.

7. Attack with a Hidden Blade

- Exercise: During a conversation, keep important information to yourself and reveal it only when it can have the most impact.

8. Borrow a Sword to Kill

- Exercise: Ask someone with specific skills to solve a problem for you, saving time and effort.

9. Advance Quickly to Secure a Position

- Exercise: Seize a sudden opportunity, like a job offer or event, by acting immediately to gain an advantage.

10. Remove the Firewood to Drown the Fish

- Exercise: Identify the weak point of a problem and work directly on it to resolve the entire issue.

11. Beat the Grass to Scare the Snakes

- Exercise: Ask a provocative question or propose an idea in a group to observe reactions and uncover others' true intentions.

12. Strike the Snake with a Stick

- Exercise: Wait for a moment when someone is vulnerable (like after a mistake) and offer your help or solution to gain an advantage.

III. Stratagems for Attack

THE 36 STRATAGEMS

When you are in a position of strength, use these stratagems to do good strategically and effectively.

13. Feign Retreat to Strike

- Exercise: In a discussion, temporarily withdraw, let the other party relax, and then resume the conversation with new arguments.

14. Flee with the Enemy in Flames

- Exercise: When facing difficulties, seek a creative alternative to escape a problematic situation instead of persisting on a path that isn't working.

15. Toss Out a Brick to Get a Jade

- Exercise: Make a small concession in a negotiation to gain something more significant in return.

16. Absorb the Energy to Take Over

- Exercise: If you receive criticism, use it to improve and demonstrate your value, turning an attack into an opportunity.

17. Toss Meat to Distract the Tiger

- Exercise: Offer a distraction or alternative when someone is focused on a problem, allowing you to resolve another important issue without interference.

18. Take a Sheep on Loan to Get Rich

- Exercise: Find a way to leverage an available resource, even a small one, to gain a benefit or advantage.

IV. Stratagems for Retreat

When you are in a position of weakness, use these stratagems to preserve your energy and continue doing good.

19. Strike at the Heart to Weaken the Spirit

- Exercise: Focus on the essentials. When you're tired, turn to acts of altruism that require less energy but have a significant impact.

20. Strategic Retreat to Maintain Strength

- Exercise: When you feel overwhelmed, take a break to recharge and return with a clearer mind.

21. Separation Tactics to Disorient the Enemy

- Exercise: If you're managing a conflict or complex project, break the problems into smaller parts and tackle them one by one.

22. Set Fire to the Enemy on All Sides

- Exercise: Approach a project or important task by managing multiple aspects simultaneously to achieve quicker and more complete results.

23. Hide the Sword in a Smile

- Exercise: Maintain a friendly attitude even when working on something critical or planning a strategic move.

24. Attack from Afar While Defending Up Close

- Exercise: Handle a difficult problem by maintaining emotional distance and seeking indirect or alternative solutions to reduce conflict.

V. Stratagems for the Melee

When you are in an uncertain position, use these stratagems to maintain balance and continue sowing goodness.

25. Pay Attention to the Enemy's Forces

- Exercise: Carefully observe the people around you, especially those who might pose a challenge or threat, to better understand their intentions.

26. Feign Confusion to Capture the Enemy

- Exercise: Pretend to be unaware or confused about a topic so others relax and reveal more than they otherwise would.

27. See the Shadow to Avoid the Knives

- Exercise: Be alert to warning signs or subtle details that might indicate an imminent problem. Anticipate and act accordingly.

28. Kill a Chicken to Scare the Monkeys

- Exercise: In a group situation, address a small problem decisively to send a strong message to others.

29. Replace the Crumbling Pillar with a New One

- Exercise: Identify a weak or ineffective part of your project or habit and replace it with something new and stronger.

30. Smile While Hiding Your True Intentions

- Exercise: Keep a positive and courteous attitude even when planning something important or confidential, so as not to raise suspicions.

VI. Stratagems for Desperation

When you find yourself in a desperate situation, use these stratagems to turn despair into an opportunity for renewal through altruism.

31. Use a Woman to Corrupt the Enemy

- Exercise: Use the power of compassion and empathy to disarm conflict. When all seems lost, a kind gesture can change the course of events.

32. Open the Door to Invite the Enemy

- Exercise: In a tense or conflictual situation, encourage the other party to dialogue or collaborate, creating an environment that seems advantageous to them but actually benefits you.

33. Retreat to Gain New Strength

- Exercise: If circumstances overwhelm you, take a step back to regain energy and motivation. Take the necessary time to reflect and restart with renewed strength.

34. Hide Behind a Smile

- Exercise: Even in extreme difficulties, maintain a positive attitude. Your smile can give hope and strength to those around you.

35. Run Away Quickly When Surrounded

- Exercise: If you find yourself in a situation with no way out or extremely unfavorable, abandon it and seek an immediate escape route without regret.

36. Stratagem of the Collapsing Tower

- Exercise: If a project or situation is doomed to fail, end it with dignity and start anew. Learn from your experience and use what you've learned to build something new and positive.

The Most Beautiful of All: Helping Others

In the end, the most powerful secret, the most beautiful stratagem of all, is unconditional altruism. Helping others not only illuminates their path but also yours. Every act of kindness, every gesture of generosity, contributes to creating a better world, one step at a time. True happiness lies in giving without expecting anything in return, in sharing the light within you to illuminate the path of others. Remember, every day is an opportunity to use the power of love and do good. This is how we can change the world together.

CONCLUSIONS / ACKNOWLEDGMENTS

As we reach the end of this journey through the ancient wisdom of the 36 Chinese stratagems, we find ourselves not at the conclusion of a path, but at the beginning of a new adventure. An adventure that, I hope, will transform the way you approach daily challenges and perceive the world around you.

Together, we have explored these 36 millennial principles, discovering how their deep understanding of human nature and power dynamics continues to resonate in our modern world. From war to love, from business to politics, from personal growth to interpersonal relationships, these stratagems offer us a lens through which to observe and navigate the complexities of contemporary life.

But the true value of this book does not lie in the mere knowledge of the stratagems.

Its potential is fully realized only through the practical application of these principles in your daily life. The 36 useful tips we have explored are just the beginning. They are seeds planted in the fertile ground of your mind, ready to germinate and flourish through your personal experience.

The practical exercises you have encountered in these pages have been designed to help you internalize these concepts, to make them an integral part of your way of thinking and acting. I encourage you to revisit these exercises regularly, constantly challenging yourself to apply these principles in new and creative ways.

Remember, true mastery lies not in memorization, but in the flexible adaptation of these principles to the unique situations you will encounter in your life. As we have seen in the shared testimonials, the creative application of these stratagems can lead to surprising and transformative results.

The secret of happiness we have explored through the prism of the 36 stratagems is not a magical formula but an invitation to live with greater awareness, flexibility, and strategic wisdom. Happiness, as we have discovered, is not a final state to be reached, but a way of navigating the sometimes tumultuous waters of life with grace, intelligence, and resilience.

As you close this book, I invite you to reflect on how you intend to integrate these teachings into your daily life. Which stratagems resonate most with you? Which challenges in your life could benefit from a more strategic approach? How can you use this wisdom not only for your personal benefit but also to positively contribute to the world around you?

Always remember that with great power comes great responsibility. Stratagems are powerful tools, and like all tools, they can be used to create or destroy. I urge you to use this wisdom with ethics and compassion, always mindful of the impact your actions have on others and the world.

This book has been a labor of love, born from a desire to make ancient wisdom accessible and relevant to the modern world. Your decision to purchase it and dedicate your precious time to its reading fills me with gratitude. I sincerely hope that you find in these pages not only knowledge but also inspiration, clarity, and, most importantly, practical tools for living a richer, more strategic, and fulfilling life.

Your journey with the 36 stratagems does not end here. In fact, it is just beginning. Every day will offer you new opportunities to practice these principles, to refine your understanding, and to discover new nuances of this ancient wisdom.

I invite you to stay curious, to continue exploring, to challenge your assumptions, and to see the world through the eyes of a strategist. Share what you have learned with others, experiment with the stratagems in your daily life, and above all, enjoy the process.

Remember, true mastery is not about controlling external events but about responding with wisdom, creativity, and flexibility to whatever life presents to you. The 36 stratagems are your compass on this journey, but the map is created by you, step by step, decision by decision.

As you move forward on your path, carry with you not only the knowledge of the stratagems but also the spirit of adaptability, creativity, and resilience that they embody. May you find in these ancient words the wisdom to navigate modern challenges, the strength to persevere in difficult times, and the inspiration to create a life rich in meaning and success.

Thank you again for embarking on this journey with the wisdom of the 36 stratagems. May it illuminate your path and guide you toward a life of fulfillment, success, and above all, happiness.

The journey continues. Wisdom is eternal. And the best is yet to come.

With deep gratitude and the best wishes for your future,

P.S. Remember, the true test of this book's value will be in its practical application in your life. Good luck, and may the wisdom of the stratagems always be with you!

FINAL TIPS AND EXERCISES

We thought there might be additional exercises for you to complete before finishing the book. Here are some practical ideas:

1. Gratitude Journal: Every day, write down three things you are grateful for and reflect on how altruism has impacted your day.

2. Kindness Week: Dedicate an entire week to performing intentional acts of kindness, such as helping a neighbor, making a donation, or writing a thank-you letter.

3. Loving-Kindness Meditation: Regularly practice a meditation focused on cultivating feelings of love and kindness toward yourself and others.

4. Community Involvement: Participate in a volunteer project in your community to put the teachings of the book into practice in the real world.

5. 36 Stratagems Challenge: For one month, choose one stratagem per day and apply it in your life to do good for yourself and others.

FEEDBACK

We would greatly appreciate your constructive feedback to help us continually improve our work. Thank you for your support.

USEFUL NOTE

We have made an effort to avoid unnecessary blank spaces between words to minimize waste and help protect Mother Earth. We hope you appreciate our commitment.

Wishing you a sincerely good life!

www.ingramcontent.com/pod-product-compliance
Lightning Source LLC
Chambersburg PA
CBHW070409230526
45471CB00006B/2720